THE DINGO

AUSTRALIAN ANIMAL DISCOVERY LIBRARY

Lynn M. Stone

Rourke Corporation, Inc.
Vero Beach, Florida 32964

PHOTO CREDITS

All photos © Lynn M. Stone

ACKNOWLEDGEMENTS

The author thanks the following for photographic assistance:
Queensland National Parks and Wildlife Service, Qld., Australia;
Northern Territory Conservation Commission, NT, Australia

LIBRARY OF CONGRESS
Library of Congress Cataloging-in-Publication Data
Stone, Lynn M.
  Dingoes / by Lynn M. Stone.

    p. cm. — (Australian animal discovery library)
    Summary: Describes the physical characteristics, behavior,
natural habitat, and relationship to humans of the Australian
wild dog known as the dingo.
    ISBN 0-86593-057-0
    1. Dingo—Juvenile literature. [1. Dingo.] I. Title.
II. Series: Stone, Lynn M. Australian animal discovery library.
QL737.C22S76   1990
599.74'442—dc20   90-30484
                                              CIP
                                              AC

Dingo

TABLE OF CONTENTS

THE DINGO

The dingo *(Canis familiaris)* is Australia's wild dog.

No one knows when or how dingoes came to Australia. Most likely, they were brought by sailors from Asia many hundreds of years ago.

The first people in Australia, the **Aborigines,** partly tamed some dingoes. Most dingoes, however, remained wild and spread throughout Australia.

Dingoes look very much like medium-sized house dogs. They howl though and sound like wolves or coyotes.

Dingo in Australia's Northern Territory

THE DINGO'S COUSINS

The dingo had already been at least partly tamed by man when it first arrived in Australia. Even today its closest relatives are **domestic** dogs. Domestic animals are those raised by man.

The dingo's closest wild relatives were probably the plains wolves of India.

Although dingoes live in the wild, they often come into contact with domestic dogs. When dingoes mate with dogs, their pups are only part dingo.

Wolf

HOW THEY LOOK

Nine of every 10 dingoes are yellowish. A few dingoes are black, white, or black and rust color.

Dingoes have a larger head than a domestic dog of the same body size. They also have longer teeth and a longer nose and jaws.

Dingoes usually have white feet and white hairs at the tip of their tail. They have pointed ears like a wolf, but not nearly so fluffy a tail.

Black Dingo

WHERE THEY LIVE

Dingoes are **adaptable.** That means they can make themselves at home in many places.

Dingoes live throughout Australia in forests, mountains, along the coasts, and on the flat, grassy plains.

In the 1920's Australians built a "dingo fence." Part of the fence has fallen apart, but it still stretches for over 3,500 miles.

The fence was supposed to keep dingoes away from many of the sheep farms. The fence did not work too well. Dingoes, it seems, already lived on both sides of the fence.

*Dingo country in
Northern Territory*

Dingo

HOW THEY LIVE

Dingoes may live alone or in groups. Groups are useful where dingoes hunt wallaroos. Wallaroos are a type of large kangaroo.

In the hottest, driest parts of Australia, dingoes are mostly **nocturnal.** That means they are active at night. During the day, they stay hidden from the sun.

In ranch country, dingoes drink from waterholes that were dug for cattle.

Dingo swimming

THE DINGO'S PUPS

A female dingo can have pups just once a year. Most domestic dogs can have two **litters** in a year.

A dingo usually has four or five pups in her litter. They are born in a cave, a hollow log, or a hole in the ground.

By the age of three or four months, the pups are old enough to be on their own.

Wild dingoes may live to be eight or 10 years old. Captives have reached nearly 15.

Young dingo at play

PREDATOR AND PREY

Like all members of the dog family, the dingo is a **predator,** or hunter. It can run fast, and it has keen ears and eyes.

The dingo usually hunts small or medium sized mammals, such as wombats, wallabies, rabbits, and wallaroos. In some places it kills lizards. The animals which the dingo hunts are its **prey.**

Dingoes also kill farm animals when they can. The dingo is not a threat to adult cattle. It does take calves, however, and sheep.

Dingo feeding

THE DINGO AND PEOPLE

Dingoes are sometimes kept as pets. They have never been truly domesticated or tamed, however. In some Australian states, it is illegal to keep dingoes.

Aborigines often live with semi-tame dingoes living nearby.

Australian sheep ranchers dislike dingoes. Dingoes sometimes kill far more sheep than they can eat. Some places in farm country pay a **bounty,** or reward money, for a dead dingo.

In some places the dingo is not hunted. People view the dingo as a helper because it kills such pests as rabbits and wild pigs.

*Golden Retriever,
a domestic dog*

THE DINGO'S FUTURE

Australia is a huge country, and much of it has not been settled by people. Many thousands of dingoes still live in wild Australia.

Dingoes have disappeared from many sheep-raising areas. The greatest threat to dingoes in the future, however, is not the farmer, but the dog.

As the number of people and dogs grows, more dingoes will mate with dogs. If each of the dingoes in Australia were someday to mate with a dog, there would soon be no more dingoes.

Many years from now, the dingo may be just another dog.

Glossary

Aborigine (ah bore IDJ in ee)—the original, or native, people of a place

adaptable (ah DAPT ah bull)—able to make changes when conditions change

bounty (BOWN tee)—a reward paid for killing or capturing certain animals

domestic (dum ES tik)—tamed and raised by man

litter (LIH ter)—a group of babies born together from the same mother

nocturnal (nohk TUR nal)—active at night

predator (PRED a tor)—an animal that kills other animals for food

prey (PREY)—an animal that is hunted by another for food

INDEX